Druidry

This book is offered with sincere and soul-deep thanks to my son Joshua, for his patience and wisdom, and to Philip Shallcrass, for being on so very many occasions my library, filled with information, laughter and affection.

I thank too all those in the tradition who spoke to me of their beliefs and practice, and answered my questions with grace and generosity.

Hail, my Lord of the Golden Wings, whose flight has carried me through these words! Hail, my Lady of the Sparkling Depths, whose bright darkness showed me the reason why! Hail, blessed ancestors, Druids of Old, may your blessings remain with these words and all who touch them.

Thorsons First Directions

Druidry

Emma Restall Orr

Thorsons
An Imprint of HarperCollinsPublishers
77–85 Fulham Palace Road
Hammersmith, London, W6 8JB

The Thorsons website address is:
www.thorsons.com

Published by Thorsons 2000

10 9 8 7 6 5 4 3 2 1

Text derived from *Principles of Druidry*, published by Thorsons 1998

Editor: Jillian Stewart
Design: Wheelhouse Creative
Photography by PhotoDisc Europe Ltd.

A catalogue record for this book
is available from the British Library

ISBN 0 0071 0336 0

Printed and bound in Hong Kong

Contents

What is Druidry?......................................2

Where Did it All Come From? 14

The Spectrum of Druidry.........................24

The Sacred Circle 34

The Magical Cycle 52

Celebration 62

The Gods 78

Useful Addresses and Further Reading 88

Druidry

is a spiritual path that honours the ancestors and the spirits of nature and celebrates individuality and creativity

What is Druidry?

If you really want to know, stop reading, just for a while.

And into a knapsack slip a little food and something to drink. Dress for the weather, taking a sweater or a waterproof if necessary. Then stop for a moment. Look around you. And, walking slowly through your home, notice everything that expresses who you are, what you have created, what is in process, what you are hoping to be, or be seen as. Notice what is of value to you and what is not. Choose something which embodies, actually or symbolically, that which you most value. You must be ready to let go of it, to give it away, yet it must mean enough to you for the act of releasing it to be profound, even difficult.

Put it into the knapsack or into your pocket, leave the house and make your way out of the buildings, the tarmac and concrete, into a landscape that is as close to the wild natural world as you can reach (yet safe enough to be in alone). Wherever it is, stay there, for a whole day, or a few days, walking, watching, feeling, sitting, listening – to yourself, to the world around you.

Listening here isn't something that can be done with any effort. It is a process of simply becoming aware, without having to react or respond. And as we listen, our bodily senses begin to awake. We start consciously to breathe through our pores, to observe and feel with our subtle body of energy. And in doing so, the effects of our presence begin to make less impact on the world around us. Spend some time listening in this way, and when you stop to eat, share your food, openly and with gratitude, by giving more than a little back to the earth, leaving a pile in a hidden place where it can be found by the little creatures or pouring a good drink into the soil or sand.

When you feel that your presence has begun gently to merge with the environment through which you wander, allow your mind to ponder upon your quest, your desire to know more about the old tradition of Druidry. What is your motivation? What do you hope to gain? What are you expecting? If you are listening with an open mind, quiet from blending your sense of self with the natural world, the answers that emerge will be your first taste of Druidry. Woven through them will be a clarity that will teach more than any written words. Through them will emerge, too, an understanding of the first step you must take on your journey into the tradition.

The time has come to leave your gift, both as an offering to the earth which nourishes you and to those who have travelled the path before you, to the Druid ancestors who will guide you upon the way. How the gift is given is up to you. It may be snuggled into the crook of a tree, thrown into water or left at a charity shop on the way home. The nature of the gift and the nature of your world, together with a little common sense and environmental sensitivity, will make the possibilities clear. The important part is the attitude with which it is given, and the letting go.

And if you don't find, in honesty, that you have reached a point where you can give your gift, consciously releasing it with thanks, then come back another day, and again and again. But don't read any more, until it is done.

The old fellow

Somewhere in our minds stands that old Druid
we have all taken on board as the original, the
prototype. He is slim, around 70, a little under
six foot tall, with long white hair, unkempt, and
a longer white beard that tapers to a point. He
is wearing a simple off-white robe with a long
dark cape around his shoulders, the loose folds
of a hood, his feet in sandals. In his hand may
be a sprig of mistletoe, a golden sickle or an
ornate wooden staff.

   The details may vary but he carries aspects of
sensitive and powerful older men who have
walked through our lives, together with images
from storybooks and cartoons we have read,
movies we have seen. Whether he is fair or
dark, the old Druid is a source of universal and
poignant wisdom. Moving with an otherworldly
serenity, he blends gentleness and age with an
absolute invulnerability.

The reality

The old fellow's strength of spirit, his certainty and flexibility, his connection with the natural world, his sensitivity and wisdom – are a powerful source of inspiration, but he is seldom an obvious presence. When we look at modern Druids, we are faced with an enormous range which is growing ever wider and richer in its variation. A Druid now is just as likely to be a woman as a man, and may come from any social, religious or educational background, may have any economic status, be of any sexuality and any race or nationality. People of every age are coming into the tradition, from the children of Druids to the oldest members of society. Urban or rural, the Druid might be an environmental lawyer, a primary school teacher, an art student, a hospital ward sister, an accountant, someone living in a twigloo on a road protest camp or running a computer systems consultancy.

So what is it that brings all these diverse people together as active students and celebrants of one tradition? What is Druidry?

The problems with finding a definition

As the number of individuals discovering Druidry grows, so too does the number of Orders and small groups, each inspired by and expressing a different facet of the tradition, each with different priorities, different spiritual and ritual textures. Within a spiritual tradition where there are so many different views it is almost impossible to find an all-encompassing definition. Groups have gathered to discuss this very issue, both seriously and with ale-fed humour, both by studying the old Irish Brehon Laws and by studying their navels. But there is simply no sacred scripture which all Druids can refer to. There is no one god, nor even one pantheon, which all Druids revere as the divine guiding force. There are no prophets who have laid down great truths together with ritual obligations – just mixtures of historical and mythical heroes.

   In many ways, Druidry is even more complex than Paganism or another broad spirituality such as Hinduism. It is a truly polytheistic faith, within which can be found space and honour for any deity or any concept of deity, together with their priests, devotees and philosophers. There are many within the tradition who call themselves

Christian, while some assert that Druidry is not a religion at all, not even necessarily a spirituality, but simply a philosophy of living.

The majority of Druids, however, are in one way or another Pagan. In making that statement, though, it is necessary to clarify Paganism as it is most widely used within the tradition. A Pagan is someone who reveres the spirits and deities of his local environment – of the earth beneath his feet, of his spring or source of water, his wood-lands and rivers, his fields and buildings, his sun and moon, and more; of everything that makes up the world that exists immediately around him.

The majority of Druids, whoever their gods may be, would accept that this is a key aspect of their practice. While some might worship the spirit of a spring, for example, as a deity, one of many gods, and others would understand the spirit to be an aspect of a higher god or creative force, any practising Druid would be sure to make offerings and prayers of thanks each time they visited that sacred place.

An Earth-ancestor spirituality

It is also possible to describe Druidry as an Earth-ancestor spirituality. The origins of the faith may be unclear, but the essence of the faith is still the honouring of the fertile Earth and the father/mother bringers of life and wisdom.

One widely accepted theory on the origin of the faith takes us back into the primitive cultures of neolithic Europe and to the motivating drive behind any religion: the need to understand the world around us in our search for survival, together with some way of assuring the future through the fertility of the land and tribe. In this, Druidry connects with all the other Earth-ancestor traditions around the globe, such as the Native American, the Maori and Huna, the Aboriginal, the Romany and the indigenous spiritualities of Africa and Asia.

Science may have given us answers to many of our forebears' questions and crises, but honouring the mysteries and manifestations of life is still a profoundly sacred and rewarding act, and it lies deep within the heart of modern Druidry.

Good boots
and a compass

Understanding Druidry in this way clarifies the honouring of the ancestors and honouring of the land as the two fundamental points of the tradition. The ancestors begin with our parents and go as far back as we can imagine. Many of us know little or nothing of our forebears, our lineage blurring beyond our grandparents, but to the Druid this is not a constraint. The ancestors exist as a people in spirit and include not only our bloodline, but also those who lived and died on the land beneath us. Our spiritual ancestry is also honoured, that is, all those who have practised within the spiritual tradition, our teachers and guides, both living and dead.

As within Druidry there is a general acceptance of the transmigration of souls, without limitation to one bloodline or one species, the act of giving to the ancestors is done with a conscious understanding that in doing so the Druid is also giving to, and honouring, the spirits of his descendants, through his blood, the Earth and the tradition.

Two effects, which in themselves are an important part of defining Druidry, emerge from the practice of honouring the ancestors and the land. The Druid will accept without reservation another person's individual experience, their perspective, their gods and their spiritual practice (so long as this does not dishonour the Earth or the ancestors): perfect tolerance. And the Druid relates to every creature, of rock or wood or leaf, the finned and feathered folk, the winged ones and the four legged, the crawlers and slitherers, the hairy, furry and smooth-skinned ones, as well as human folk, primarily as spirit and therefore with an equal right to life, respect and dignity: perfect equality.

Understanding these elements, the land and the ancestors, as two powerful basics of modern Druidry, perhaps we can stop for a moment. Think about them. How much do you honour your parents? What do you know of your blood ancestors and of the ancestors of the Earth beneath your feet? In what way do you or could you honour them, acknowledging their spirit, their experience, their gifts? And what of the teachers who have been your guides, with lessons that were hard as well as those where you succeeded?

What too of your attitude towards the Earth? Think about how you have received from the Earth and in what way you have given thanks for that, in what way you have consciously reciprocated, giving back.

Then slide those basics on, as if they were sturdy walking boots, and tie the laces well. As you travel into the tradition, they will give you sure footing. And looking up at the road ahead, take as a compass the tenets of tolerance and equality. They will bring you back to the path, should doubt cloud your way.

The journey

My first suggestion was to stop reading, to get out of our civilized world and find the world of nature where the vibrations of humanity are not omnipresent. In your wilderness you gave an offering of yourself, expressing your commitment to discover more. Such offerings blend our celebration of who we are and what we have been given with our willingness to sacrifice something of ourselves, and they help us to see more clearly both what we have and how we are willing to change.

It is in the arms of nature, in the colours of the sunset, in the thoughts that glide through us as we watch the horizon through the grass, feeling the Earth beneath our body, listening, awake, that the spirit of Druidry glows. The Earth itself, with the tides and cycles of nature, is the holy scripture of the tradition and the source of our understanding of it. These words are no more than a rough map and field guide, with ideas about what might be seen along the way.

There is no need to struggle to believe in anything, nor to love and follow blindly. Druidry is a spiritual journey of the individual's soul, one that honours each unique vision and expression.

Who might we meet along the way?

Any path into Druidry will at some stage lead the traveller to encounter other Druids and seekers. Treading the path alone is often a necessary stage of the journey, but to join others can be both rewarding and instructive.

While those the traveller might meet may come from any part of the spectrum of Druidic expression, they may also be working on very different levels within the tradition. The mystical spirituality at the core of Druidry is a place of profound personal dedication which inspires the Druid to focus his whole life into his faith. Around the core exists the wider community of Druidry where the intensity and discipline are not so demanding and this group includes many who simply want to learn a little more, to gather together to celebrate the festivals and rites, and strive to live by Druidic principles.

Whoever we meet, it is worth remembering that any individual, in body or in spirit, does not represent any other part of the tradition or the community other than themselves.

Where does the path go?

Druidry is a sacred journey of discovering the beauty and sanctity of all life, both physical and spiritual. Yet it is not enough for the Druid simply to know that all creation is sacred: the path leads beyond that point to a place where they can feel the touch of the gods by reaching into the spirit that vitalizes the world.

One of the keys of the tradition is the *awen*. This is an old Welsh word which can be translated as 'flowing spirit' and is understood to mean the flow of divine inspiration which comes at that point of exquisite contact, pouring out from a deity and into a Druid. With the inspiration comes the energy, the empowerment needed for the Druid to allow that sacred inspiration to pour through them into creativity.

The nature of the creativity inspired by this blissful connection with the divine can come in many forms, according to the skills of the individual, his own needs or those of the person or people for or with whom he is working. Poetry and music, the telling of stories and magical myths are the most commonly associated works of creative expression that emerge out of Druidry.

Where Did It All Come From?

Let us begin our journey by stopping, as we step onto the path, and looking out over the landscape from which that path emerged. It is not possible to see the path as one unbroken track all the way back to the distant horizon. For those entering an old tradition with great enthusiasm reined to the belief that there is a strong and continuous line from ancient Druidry to the present day, being faced with this broken path can be disenchanting. Yet Druidry exists as a growing tradition. How can this be so?

The sources

From prehistory there is virtually no evidence that might allow us to piece together the spiritual practices of these islands. Despite the wealth of New Stone Age and Bronze Age sites scattered over the land, there is nothing from that period that gives any true clarity in terms of deities revered or ceremonies performed. With the spread of Iron Age culture across Europe we find a little more, but it is not until the Romans arrived in the first century BCE that a clearer picture emerges about the religions of these lands. Yet as Druidry has long been connected with Celtic culture, Classical sources tend to have been overlooked in favour of medieval Irish and Welsh literature and, for some Druids, the work of eighteenth and nineteenth-century scholars.

Yet Druidry is not necessarily based on any of these sources. As a spirituality deeply rooted in the land, it has evolved through the needs of the land and the people who have relied upon that land, shifting, adapting, balancing just as our environment does. Viewing the landscape and various stretches of track in search of the nature of the tradition, what appears most important is not the continuity but the colours, the detail and images that catch our eye.

The earliest traces

The earliest images date back to a time when the climate of Britain became gradually warmer and the period which we call the neolithic began. This provided the first evidence of a spiritual practice. The neolithic long barrows, chambered passage graves dating as far back as 4400 BCE, are now thought to be the oldest human-made monuments on Earth. Though thousands still exist across western Europe, each one differs sufficiently to blur any attempts to focus on a pattern. The energy of these graves is rich, dark, earthy, born out of a time with few certainties when the world was vast, and nature wild and hungry. Any measure of understanding that the priests of the time had about the mysteries of the stars, the seasons and tides, the patterns of growth, the movements of the wild herds, about birth and death, would have been deeply honoured. Those who held the knowledge, however sketchy or superstitious, would have been revered – and feared.

Around 3200 BCE the old long barrows were carefully blocked up – perhaps to seal in the power of the old ancestral spirits, perhaps to ensure they were not disturbed, perhaps through fear – and circular bank and ditch earthworks constructed. In Ireland and the north-west reaches of Britain, some of the old barrows were built upon with new tombs, creating developed passage graves such as Newgrange, implying that here there was a different attitude towards the older religion.

Many of the bank and ditch structures developed into circles of wooden poles and, later, stones. Some of these have survived or been recreated, such as the huge Avebury ring in Wiltshire. The priests of these people would have had a very different task from those of the earlier neolithic period. The climate was warm and the energy or atmosphere of these sites is lighter, more open.

The circle era is thought to have come to an end around 1200 BCE, when the circles were abandoned due, it appears, to a deterioration in the weather. The temperature had suddenly begun to fall, reaching its lowest point around 1000 BCE. The clear skies and starry nights which so beautifully attuned with the stone temples built out on the moors and meadows were a thing of the past. It rained – and with no clear predictability in the weather, any solar, lunar or stellar alignments in a temple or tomb became a virtual irrelevance.

The spiritual focus shifted to the new elemental force which was driving through the lives of the people: water. Archaeological evidence now reveals for us the wealth of metal-work, jewellery and weaponry that was offered into rivers, lakes and wells at this time, as the people called out to the spirits of the water.

Take some time and go to an ancient long barrow or course of water or circle. If there are none accessible, take yourself there in your imagination. Either way, be sure to take with you an offering for the spirits, for the ancestors, their gods and the guardians of the site. Remember that offerings should be quickly biodegradable or edible for local wildlife; ideally there should be no trace left after just a few days.

Before you approach the site, sit quietly and relax, calming yourself to a point where you will be able to listen. Then, quietly and with respect, walk around the site staying relaxed, listening. Allow impressions of the place to seep into your senses. What would have been the role of the priest at the time the site was built or used as a place of worship? What were the needs of the people? What of the needs of the land?

Present your offerings, in peace and with thanks, before you leave, disconnecting from the site with respect.

Who were the Celts?

It is often declared that Druids were the priesthood of the Celtic people. If this was so, where are the Celts in the changing colours and climate of these islands?

The term *Keltoi* was first used by Greek historians writing in the fifth century BCE to refer to some of the peoples living north of the Alps. It was this reference that archaeologists of the last century recalled when uncovering evidence of a tribal culture in early Iron Age Austria. The finds – bronze objects and pictures inscribed on pottery – give us an impression of the lifestyle, with representations of what could be seen to be musicians, Bards, dancers, priest figures and deities.

The culture spread. The first traces are found in southern Britain from the early sixth century BCE and thereafter it appeared to move slowly south-west to the Iberian peninsula, eastwards to Turkey and north to Scotland and Ireland. When Julius Caesar referred to the *Celtae*, 400 years after the Greeks, he was describing a people of central and southern France. It's difficult then to be distinct about who the Celts were. Celtic culture is simply that of the Iron Age people of Europe.

The classical sources

The writings of Roman warriors and historians give us the first evidence (if politically biased) of the ancient religions. The picture they paint is of Druids being an educated élite, influential in political and legal affairs, in philosophy, history and learning, healing and magic, as well as overseeing or carrying out religious ceremonial.

Julius Caesar was one of the first to write of Druids, in the first century BCE, and was one of the few who actually knew a Druid: the tribal chief Divitiacus. It is through Caesar's work that we first find the Gallic word 'Druid'. The origins of the word itself, however, are debated. It is generally thought that the first part comes from the word for 'oak', which in many European languages is close to *drui*. The latter part may come from the Indo-European root word *wid*, meaning 'wisdom'. The Druid then is suggested to be the one who holds the wisdom of the oak.

The piecing together of information on the ancient religions is necessary because Druidry was an oral tradition. The Druids never wrote down any aspect of their religion. One reason for this was, no doubt, to reduce the risk of their teachings being desecrated and misused, but also, as an oral tradition, it held in highest esteem the power of the mind and of memory.

The Romans' contribution

The Romans did attempt to eradicate the Druids, yet it was not their religion which threatened the polytheistic and Pagan Roman imperialists, but the political power which they held over the tribes. The Romans didn't come for the purpose of settling, they came to take control, and everything of value to each British kingdom, their natural and human resources, trade links and knowledge, was overseen by the Druids. It isn't surprising, then, that the Druids were often at the heart of insurrections against the conquering armies.

As the Roman forces moved across Britain, the influence of the Druids diminished. Their role was never quite the same again, although in Ireland and the farthest reaches of Scotland, which the Romans never reached as a conquering army, their work did continue.

In terms of sources for modern Druids to understand their spiritual ancestry, the Romans did not only leave their writings, but also pictures and inscriptions about the nature of the gods – not just those they brought with them but also the local deities. It is through these inscriptions that modern Druids are discovering the names of some of the older gods.

The medieval tales

With the Druids' influence diminished under first Roman rule, then the tyranny of Christianity, the essence of the faith survived most strongly through the art and craft of the Bards. The first written source for the Druid tradition from a non-Classical origin dates from the late sixth century onwards: the medieval Bardic literature of Wales and Ireland.

Bards were a part of the Druid caste and their role was to affirm the identity of the tribe and the strength of the king, often with genealogies that reached back to the gods. The Bards were deemed no threat to the Roman invaders, and they continued as entertainers and storytellers, now not only keeping the wisdom of their craft but also carrying much of the Druid wisdom, wrapped in a different cloth.

By the sixth century the Saxons, Angels and Jutes were moving west in search of land on which to settle, and those who could not or would not tolerate the change were being driven west before them. This evoked two strands of interest: first, from those incomers who were curious about the culture which their presence was diluting; and second, from within these people themselves who felt a rising need to preserve that culture. The stories, poetry and songs dating from this time are not a pure rendition of the old Bardic tales and are written with a distinct if beautifully creative overlay of both Graeco-Roman influences and Christianity. For many modern Druids, however, these tales are of exquisite value as sources of their own spiritual inspiration and are not diminished in value because of the mix of cultures. They are another expression of the evolution of a spirituality which honours creativity and the gods of all creation.

So the historical sources of Druidry are not entirely clear. Yet the tradition offers the person who stands looking back for inspiration thousands of places to dive in and breathe deeply. And if we understand Druidry to be a spirituality whose focus is the search for divine and perfect inspiration, we must also accept that each soul will find that source in her own way.

The Spectrum of Druidry

Within modern Druidry there is a wide spectrum of belief and practice. For the newcomer to the faith, any personal inkling about what Druidry is might be entirely thwarted by encountering one Druid and warmly affirmed in meeting another. Yet the desire to find others who share similar perspectives, with its potential for spiritual kinship and the intimacy of common experience, does bring people together.

By looking at these shared perspectives we can define some distinct groups, though it must be understood that individuals are likely to meander across any boundaries I may suggest.

The strength of the Celtic

Though the Iron Age Celtic peoples may be the first culture of these lands that left enough evidence for us to grasp any idea of their ways of life, it is the medieval Irish and Welsh texts that have had the most direct influence on wide areas of modern Druidry.

To understand these stories and poems we must go to the texts themselves. Nowadays there is a good range in various translations. Another useful guide is to look back at the way in which the Bardic tradition may have developed.

As a part of the Druid caste the Bards were supported by their communities. While the Druid held the power, performing ceremonies and rites as judge priest and magician, the role of the Bard was quite different. It was his task to know by heart the histories of the people and the land, and to recite these for the tribal king or chief, or any who would pay. The Bard was the force that gave the people their identity. It is understood that the novice began training as a Bard and progressed through the Ovate stage, where divination and healing become important, to become a Druid. These three groups remain the most widespread in the modern tradition.

When the influence of the Druids was diminishing under repression, some of their old wisdom was robed in the Bardic tradition, held in the stories, the myths of the people and their land. For some modern Druids these tales are a source of profound guidance and spiritual inspiration. In many ways they act as a link between the twenty-first century and the pre-Christian Druids.

There is an element within modern Druidry that craves this sense of Celtic identity. In the search for self, for belonging, for roots, there are many who seek the Celtic and do so in the most part through the medieval literature. Finding inner strength through a personal connection with an ancient heritage can be an important part of the journey, offering that intimacy of shared experience and community of spirit which is felt to be deeply rooted, whether the individual has a blood link to a modern Celtic land or merely a soul allegiance.

There are also those within the faith for whom the journey is an intellectual quest to discover the authentic nature of Druidry. These Druids mainly reject any work later than the medieval texts, which they use very specifically, extracting what is useful and relevant to our era and creating a modern Druidry that is deemed to have an authentic ancient base.

A greater proportion of those within the Druid tradition relate to the Celtic literature as works of creativity, not potential sources of authenticity, content that modern Druidry needs no validation from the past, having evolved naturally into its present state, always existing on the inner planes.

In these various ways modern Druids walk a path that leads them to the spirit of the Celtic people, or what is felt to be the embodiment of all that is Celtic: the Celtic deities. Not all Druids hold Celtic gods as their principal deities, yet the Celtic is widely acknowledged and honoured as a key influence in the evolution of these lands and the development of the faith.

Read some of the old Irish and Welsh stories (suggestions can be found on page 90), getting a feel for both cultures and the differences and similarities between them. If the opportunity arises, hear a modern Bard telling the stories, perhaps in a traditional way, accompanied by a harp. Do they awake some part of your soul with a deep familiarity? Does the Irish feel more comfortable or the Welsh?

Choose one story and read it again and again. What does this story say to you, what does it teach you? How? Recite it aloud. Take it to a place that seems appropriate to the story, perhaps by a river, a hazel tree, a well, and tell it again there. Allow it to slip into your memory. How does it feel to hold it now inside you?

The Christian angle

A significant proportion of Druids do not identify themselves as primarily Pagan. There are those who declare Druidry is not a spirituality or religion, and many hold that it is a path of mysticism, a wisdom school, within which one can hold any religious belief. A good number of these non-Pagans blend the philosophies of Druidry with those of Christianity.

For a Druid Christian, the Earth and all creation is an expression of the deity as presence, and therefore deeply sacred. While there are Christians who acknowledge this without moving into Druidry, others find that the philosophy significantly strengthens and broadens their faith. In an age when environmentalism, the importance of family and community, interest in folk traditions and natural medicine are all increasing, the point at which Druidry and Christianity meet becomes clearer. For the wider Pagan and polytheistic Druid community, these Christic Druids (and those who blend Druidry with other religions) are acknowledged and respected simply as revering another of the numerous gods.

Anglo-Saxon and Nordic influences

For some modern Druids the old Celtic culture and the medieval literature have no direct influence on their faith whatsoever. Instead of moving back to the Celtic as a source of their Druidry, they acknowledge the later Anglo-Saxon settlers, studying their Germanic language, deities, myths and poems, and their magical tradition.

The understanding is that, if Druids were the priesthood of the Celtic people – who were the Iron Age Europeans – then the Saxons were simply a later version of the Celts. The Saxons who invaded Britain from the fifth century were still Pagan, while the Celtic kings had been Christianized, giving another reason for those who take this path to work within it.

The Anglo-Saxon influence was not the only one which spread into these lands during the medieval period. The Nordic religions of the Danes, the Vikings, also made its impact, and though most who revere the Nordic gods do so through the Icelandic Asatru or Odinistic religions, there are also Druids whose principal inspiration comes through these threads.

The romantic revival

A large swathe of modern Druidry is influenced by the Druid revival of
the eighteenth century. From the sixteenth century there came an
increasing interest in antiquarianism. As the eighteenth century
dawned, a romantic ideal of our ancient roots was being nurtured,
adorned with art, poetry and music.

  A new Celtic spirit was being stirred up, and enthusiasm for ancient
and cultural history was growing. The medieval literature was also
becoming more widely available and provided inspiration for one
Edward Williams (Iolo Morgannwg) to piece together all he could find
about the ancient tradition, adding, where necessary, forged
documents. In 1792 Morgannwg assembled the first gorsedd (or
gathering) of Bards of the Isle of Britain. A great deal of the ritual
he devised is still used today.

Mythical heroes

For some in the tradition, history is a confusing mixture of fact and attitude, and felt to be best ignored in favour of the tales which appear to hold the true power of the land and the human soul. While some dive back into the Celtic past for these tales, others prefer the kick and wit of the Arthurian sagas. To a lesser extent the other tales of our culture, such as those of Robin Hood, work within Druidry in the same way as the Arthurian.

In all these tales we can find examples of every aspect of human nature, and the Druid who walks into the inner worlds where the stories are played out in a thousand different colours and chords can merge into the characters, the landscape and the emotion, reworking the quests according to his own soul.

Not only do the stories allow us a better understanding of ourselves through whatever type of psychoanalysis we naturally employ, they also offer to the Druid archetypes of strength, glory, salvation, integrity, pride, dedication, love and more. They express a devotion to the land, to the people, in a way which is easily accessible on many levels.

Environmentalists

Those within the tradition who are passionately involved in the protection of the environment come in many shapes and colours, from the road protester to the organizer of an environmental awareness group or lobby to those working directly within the law on issues of pollution or development.

All within Druidry do work for the environment. For some the focus is local, for some it is global. Some are happy on a protest march, others dancing a rite within their sacred circle. However the Druid is involved, the key tenets of his faith will always guide him: we are all spirit, equal and connected.

And all filled with awen

 The only kind of Druid not yet mentioned is the hereditary, one who claims to be of a family line through which the ancient wisdom was never lost. Whether these lines go back 40 generations or four is usually impossible to validate. It would be disrespectful to try.

Within Druidry there is no sure way of knowing whether an individual is genuine, trained and true. Few colleges or teachers issue certificates of membership, of courses completed or validated genealogies, simply because these would mean so little anyway. Becoming a Druid is a life-long task. Indeed, many say that the work of being a Druid is a constant process of becoming, of reaching the archetype of strength, wisdom, clarity, invulnerability and gentle humanity, together with an understanding of nature at its rawest edges. We stretch through our souls to the essence of life, to the spirit that vitalizes, to the gods that empower us, in search of inspiration.

Perhaps the only clear measure of a Druid, accepting that he honours the Earth and the ancestors, is in the expression of his *awen*.

The Sacred Circle

To offer an idea of what Druids do is a plan thick with complications. How could I possibly within these few pages reveal the nature, the flavour, the colour of every variation?

As a guide I can walk only one path at a time, though along the way I can point out other paths visible to me. The track I take is in the main that of my own Druidic practice and it is the widest track, along which the majority have made their way over the past 20 years.

Healing and connectedness

Two clear motivations arise when looking at the reasons why people move into the Druid tradition. The first is healing, the second connectedness. The potential for healing is deep and powerful within Druidry. The tradition offers an extraordinary level of inner certainty, easing any physical dis-ease or mental/emotional instability through finding a deeper sense of peace and self-confidence. Instead of focusing on the need for spiritual transcendence, the Druid perspective takes us in search of spirit, the energy within the physical that shines with life. The desire is to find the point of balance, not necessarily to ensure we remain at that place, but to give us a balanced perspective and the ability to restabilize after an adventure off centre.

As a journey of self-discovery, Druidry offers us tools to understand not only the overt sides of our nature, but also the underlying beliefs which affect us so strongly and often detrimentally. In the process of changing our attitude towards the world around us, learning to acknowledge its spiritual essence and beauty, we also discover the strength and beauty within ourselves.

Sacred time, sacred space

Many begin their path by creating an altar. Determining a certain place within the house or room as sacred and committing to spend time there in lives which are too busy and distracted confirms our dedication to the path. We are giving not only to all those whom we would honour at the altar, but also to ourselves.

The art of creating and tending an altar is an important part of Druidry. It need not be big, but big enough for a candle or two and the other bits and pieces. It may even be in the garden or in a secluded spot in the wild beyond.

With the candles place offerings which represent for you the beauty and strength in your life, all you would give thanks for and to, the natural world and the ancestors. It isn't necessary to make it all at once: allow it to evolve and beautiful objects to present themselves. These may be stones, shells, feathers, cones, photos of your family, a chalice of water, a bowl of earth.

The altar should be tended daily. You may bring to the altar flowers, foliage or fresh fruit, a hunk of bread, a little of your meal. With the candles lit, spend a period of time quietly before it. You may like to meditate, but the important part is to stop running, to relax, to ponder on the beauty and simply to be, for a short while, every day.

Water should be refreshed daily and any fresh food and flowers replaced when necessary (composting what you remove or leaving it in a secluded place for the wildlife outside).

Of the sea-washed pebbles on the beach, the one we have chosen for our altar is no more blessed than the others, no more an expression of divine creation, yet picking one up, touching its smoothness, feeling its beauty, is an act of devotion, whether we understand it to have been created by a god, a natural force or a tangle of energy held within the hands of a thousand gods and spirits. Our gift to that creative force is the moment of awe which flows through us when we open our senses to the wonder of nature. Our altar is an expression of that wonder. So creating and working with an altar also begins the shift towards the key tenet within Druidry: that all is sacred.

The altar focuses our quest onto the natural world, but not without acknowledging the human element. As the Druid listens to the rocks and trees, she is also listening to the hum in the air, the shimmer of light and breath that holds the stories and memories of those who have walked the land before. Knowing that the soul is conscious between lives and actively chooses the time, place and circumstances of birth, the Druid honours her parents as souls she has chosen to work with, in order to learn and grow. Our children in turn have chosen us. At difficult times in relationships the altar can be a reminder of the gifts we have been given, the opportunities for learning. Lighting a candle for our ancestors is a potent tool for healing.

The animistic vision, which sees all aspects of the created world alive with spirit, does not mean for all Druids that each stone has its gnome, each tree its dryad. The important element is the way in which all things are connected. Every thought and action sends shivers of energy into the world around us, which affect all creation. Perceiving the world as a web of connectedness helps us to overcome the feelings of separation that hold us back and cloud our vision. This connection with all life increases our sense of responsibility for every move, every attitude, allowing us to see clearly that each soul does indeed make a difference to the whole.

Druid ritual

The sacred space of the altar and the time we spend in tending it is further extended when we look at ritual.

   Ritual, playing out a prayer with a physical action, is significant. Informal ritual is a part of daily life, honouring with thanks and awe the beauty of nature, bowing with reverence to the moon as it rises, saluting the sun and stars, greeting the trees, offering thanks for food and water, blessing a soul in distress. The moments are numerous, the actions a natural response, yet often performed in a certain way, according to how the individual was taught. Where others are present ritual shows what is being done, even if words are not spoken, but more importantly it moves the body through which the energy needs to flow and through movement the subconscious mind registers change.

   The ability to perform ritual more formally is an important part of the Druid's training. Within the framework of ceremony, mind and energy are concentrated and therefore stronger. A dance of words and movement is crafted which enchants the gods, evoking curiosity within the worlds of spirit, and creating opportunities for whatever transformation and regeneration are required.

The call for peace

Before any formal ritual, a call is made for peace. Addressing the four compass directions, the Druid establishes that there is peace, and if she is not alone she will also address the gathering as a whole. Why this is done has half a dozen answers, historical, traditional, romantic and psychological, as do most questions about modern Druidry.

When we call to the north, the south, east and west, 'Let there be peace!' it is a demand on our own ability both to perceive the world around us with fuller awareness and to pour into the world the beauty of peace. And, as around us, so within: the call for peace is a reminder to let go of the crises of conflict in our daily lives as we move into the sacred space of the circle.

The call for peace, then, is the first and encompassing intention of any Druid rite.

The circle cast

Most formal ritual is performed within a circle that is cast and consecrated. This is the temple of the Druid. The circle is drawn on the earth or in the air, its ceiling the sky, the clouds, the trees' canopy. Many circles are cast in the same place, again and again. The most established are set with trees or stones. Many Druids, though, will cast a circle and perform their rite, and when the circle is uncast, no trace will be left but the energy of the ceremony shimmering. But the circle is more than simply an area marked out in which to work.

In a place where you will not be disturbed, stand with sufficient space around you to stretch. Breathe deeply a few times, relaxing, finding your natural balance. Then bring your focus gently to the centre of that balance. In your own time, start to sense with your breathing the extent of your own space, your private space. Some would call this the emotional body, a layer of the aura, the area around you in which you don't like strangers to linger. It is your safe space. Trace its edge with your mind, then with a finger outstretched.

With the rhythm of your breath extend that circle, pushing it out in every direction. It may be easy, or it may take time to find the right 'muscle'. Don't go further than is comfortable, returning often to the centre point of your balance, affirming the circle as your safe space. When you are ready, breathe it back to its original size. This may be easier, or harder than extending it.

A shared circle is also a place of absolute trust, a trust that is based on the harmony between every soul present. Where there are people who don't know each other, it is the role of the Druid leading the rite to ensure that the sense of trust is shared. The act of casting the circle is an important part of this.

This is done in a number of different ways, depending on how the Druid perceives reality. By moving around the circle in a sunwise (clockwise) direction, using a pointed finger, a wand, sword or sacred knife, the Druid delineates its edge by projecting light or colour, usually of white, silver, gold or blue. More shamanically, by seeing the threads of the web of connectedness, in casting the circle the Druid will sever those threads, to refasten them again once the rite is done.

Either way, the cast circle is cut off from the world, a bubble that exists outside time and space, a perfect sanctuary. Within the circle there is no distraction or threat from the world outside, but equally importantly, the world outside is not affected by events within it.

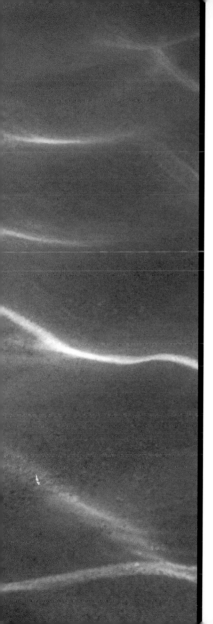

Consecration

The temple of the sacred circle is usually consecrated, using incense and water which together represent the four elements the Druid works with. Within the incense is *earth*, in the dried herbs and berries, resin, bark and oils that make up the mixture that is burnt, expressing the *fire*, sending plumes of beautiful smoke into the *air*, to be breathed by the wind and the circle's participants. The *water* is often from a sacred spring, but always it is fresh, representing the waters of life. At times the chalice may have herbs or petals infusing their essence into the water.

When the circle is consecrated, the Druid calls to her gods, the elementals, the devas of the Earth, to bless the smoking censer and the chalice, then, as she moves slowly sunwise, letting the incense swirl, scattering water with fingertips, there is a shift in the energy and the vibration changes. The fifth element, *spirit*, comes into play. The circle, blessed, is ready for the rite.

Holding the bubble

Working within a circle that is altogether detached from the Earth can be useful, at times, but is not the usual way within Druidry. The bubble freely floating is transcendent of the manifest world and only with lifetimes of discipline is the mind able to perfect such a temple.

In Druidry, we bring into our temple our memories and expectations, and the bubble is held by our reverence for the world in which we live.

The Druid begins by honouring the four directions. Merely by looking at the geographic quarters – north, south, east and west – our world is created in our minds. Cultures, climates, nations and races, heat and cold, serenity and pollution, animals, colours, deserts, seas, memories of love and pain and more, all are evoked at the mention of these words. Each image rests at the edge of our focus, ready to be used.

Take a piece of paper and a pen. Work out the directions, using the sun or a compass if necessary. For a few minutes stand facing east, working out what of the Earth lies before you, which countries, which bodies of water, mountain ranges, flora, fauna, cultures. Let your mind wander there. What do you smell? What do you feel?

Write down what you perceive and move on to the next quarter.

There are no defined correspondences here, for each individual has a unique perception of the world. The calls that are made to the quarters reflect that unique vision. They are not a demand for presence or protection, but a greeting, an invitation.

Most in the tradition in Britain work with the four elements in the same places around the circle, with earth in the north, air in the east, fire in the south and water in the west. The calls often reflect these aspects of our world too, so a call to the east might be:

> To the spirits of the wild wind and all those who fly free upon her breath, I call to you! Feathered ones, sacred hawk, flying high on mountain air! Honoured trees who offer us our every breath of life! We ask you that you do bless this rite, in the name of the Old Gods.

Once the directions have been honoured, in many Druid circles the spirits of nature are more specifically acknowledged, with offerings being given. The ancestors may be called, the teachers and guides who exist in spirit, with offerings of music, song, dance and drums, or a libation of wine or mead, the lighting of a candle.

Then into the temple the Druid will invoke their gods.

Druidry works as a profoundly grounded spirituality. Reverence for the natural world allows the mind and the soul to venture into the worlds of spirit knowing where it is coming from. The circle, detached from the mundane yet honouring the Earth, allows those within it to discover and affirm their strength, establish their centre, deepen their awareness of themselves and their creativity, their blocks and vulnerabilities. Rooted and blessed, reaching into the essence of life from that sacred safe space on the quest for divine inspiration, the *awen* which will pour through our bodies and souls, the spirit can truly soar.

When the ritual is completed, the devotions made and thanks given, any energy vibrant within the circle is directed according to the purpose of the rite (or some other cause) through the focus of a prayer. One often used is, 'May the world be filled with love, peace and harmony.' When the circle is uncast, the energy will flow according to the intent of that prayer.

The inner and outer grove

As well as the sacred temple in the wildwood, the individual working within the Druid tradition will also discover another grove within the inner worlds of the mind. Some perceive this to be merely imagination, while others assert that it exists in its own right on a different layer of reality. Either way, the time spent in this grove is an important part of the Druid's work.

If we consider this to happen only in the psyche, by delving deep into the imagination to discover/create an inner temple grove we are developing the powers of our mind, expanding our ability to visualize. Both for creativity and healing, indeed any magical process, these are essential skills, and the more the student works within her inner grove, discovering its every detail, the stronger and clearer her spiritual path becomes. The grove, like the sacred circle, is a perfect sanctuary, and finding the inner grove establishes a place which is always calm and nourishing, soul deep. Interaction with the gods and the faeryfolk, the ancestors and spirit teachers is for most people considerably easier on this inner level.

If we believe that the inner grove exists on another level of reality, every moment spent in this otherworld increases the student's knowledge and ability to function on different planes of consciousness, sliding in spirit between realities. What is gained from working on other levels differs according to the soul and the intent, but the keys are finding a radical angle of perception and potential for change.

Most who study Druidry find themselves a grove outside, too. Whether they drift out there every twilight, once a moontide or twice a year, simply being out in the arms of nature, amongst the trees and in a sacred circle, is a feast to the soul.

Trees have always been important in the Druid tradition. If we slip back to an age when there were vast and ancient trees, with nothing bigger but the hills, when wood was the only source of fuel and shelter, we start to understand the reverence our ancestors had for them.

Find a tree you feel comfortable to be with, ideally in a quiet spot where you will be undistracted. Remember to take offerings with you.

As you approach the tree, stop at the edge of the canopy and find once again the circle of your aura, centred in your spirit. Ask permission of the dryad before you walk into the circle of the tree. When you feel your presence has been accepted, walk slowly, aware of your energy weaving with that of the tree, circling around the trunk, spiralling in, until you find a place by the trunk appropriate for you to stay. Relax. Listen.

Then ask the dryad if it would be acceptable for you to raise your awareness of its being. If you feel the answer to be yes, find your balance, affirm your own circle, now interwoven with the tree spirit, lean back against the tree and close your eyes. Allow your consciousness to slide down through your body into your feet. Feel the energy of the earth holding you as it does the tree. Slip further, into the earth, so that you might feel the roots spreading out in the dark soil, drinking in moisture, holding stones, sheltering creatures. Feel the energy of the nourishment invigorating your spirit, and when you are filled let your consciousness rise up through your body, through the strength of your trunk and up into your arms, reaching out like branches into the air, up to the sky, towards the light, unfurling leafbuds. Feel the sun on your face, the wind in your leaves.

When you are ready, slip down with your mind into the centre of your body. There, feel the balance, between Earth and sky, between sunlight and dark earth, affirming your roots, celebrating your branches, and give thanks.

Returning to your normal consciousness, give your offerings and thanks to the tree spirit. When you leave, detach consciously from its energy as you move out from its sacred circle of canopy and roots. Affirm your own sacred circle, your strength and connectedness.

Ogham

Ogham is a sacred alphabet used widely within modern Druidry, where each of the 25 letters corresponds to a different tree or plant. Originating from southern Ireland, it dates, some claim, from 600 BCE, but there is no evidence it is any older than second century CE.

There is healthy debate as to what exactly the 25 trees and plants are. What is agreed is that each letter represents not only a tree or plant, but also a whole store of other associations, allowing the alphabet to work as a series of mnemonics. Within it are allusions to season, colour, sound, landscape, herbs, birds, insects and other wildlife, healing and toxins. Through the natural history of the trees and ancient myths, the alphabet alludes to the history of the land and its people.

Many Druids feel ogham existed as an initiatory mystery, giving their ancient counterparts a way of communicating without being understood by non-initiates. With its many layers of meaning the ogham alphabet is used for the most part by modern Druids as a tool for divination, each letter opening doorways into other worlds. In the same way that runes work, their shapes can be found in landscapes, or the presence of a certain tree or plant can be understood as revealing messages and omens.

Drugs and medicine

The use of herbs and trees for healing, for shifting consciousness and changing the level of energy vibration is widespread in modern Druidry, with a significant number in the tradition qualified to work as practitioners of herbal medicine. Many more use herbs in preference to manufactured drugs and remedies. With an attitude that honours each plant and tree as having its own deva or dryad, the soul seeking guidance, change or healing will primarily address the spirit, interacting on that level before any part of the plant or tree is physically taken or consumed. The use of illegal drugs is not encouraged in any part of modern Druidry, not even the shamanic. Trance states and ecstasy can be reached using just the powers of the mind.

The Magical Cycle

When Druids gather together their group is called a Grove, whether they meet in the forest, on the moors or in an urban setting. The Grove is a circle of souls, each honoured as individual yet sharing a common source of nourishment in the rich and fertile earth, sharing aims of growth and fruition.

Change

Change can be stressful, whether it is part of the natural process of growth and decay or something we have worked on through our creativity, our search for healing, knowing and letting go. With its focus on the natural world, its constant and inevitably changing tides, Druidry offers a tool not only for coping with change but also for thriving on it.

The Druid's sacred circle is, as we have seen, painted with the colours of his world, from his immediate environment to the global geography and the universe. Though these shift and change, they are relatively still for us: trees and mountains, oceans, nations, climates. These hold us, becoming part of our perception and understanding of our world, and how within that world we can create a sanctuary, dedicated to all that has made us who we are, all that nourishes and guides us to become all that we could be …

Into the circle are then added those elements of life which are constantly changing, all that provokes and guides us to change ourselves. The Druid temple becomes a sanctuary where change itself is blessed and contained within safe space.

Cycles of time

Our ancestors watched the skies with awe, tracking the path of the sun, seeing how it changed through the year, observing and learning to work with the effects it had on their environment. The Druid too watches the sun's path with awe. Our science may fractionally explain it, but we are still dependent on its continuity. Its path creates day and night and, in temperate lands, the seasons of the year.

It is our perception of these cycles that we use with the sacred circle, painting their changing colours onto the landscapes that are already there. So in the north of our circle, for instance, we acknowledge the night and all that 'night' means to us. In the north too we find winter, its cold and darkness. The seasons not only find expression in the trees, the plants, the physicality of existence, but impact equally strongly upon our human psyche. In Druidry it is understood that the more closely we follow the prompts of nature, releasing to the changes within ourselves, the healthier we can be. Ignoring the flows of change builds up stress and retains blinkers which deny us clarity and strength. Beyond the desire for well-being, it is in attuning with the cycles of each day and season that we discover doorways into deeper knowing, making connections with the forces of nature and the gods.

Where you will be undistracted, mark out a circle on the ground, physically or with your imagination. Standing in its centre, breathe gently, fully, until you are relaxed, then extend your aura until it fills the circle. Feeling its strength, the centredness of your spirit, walk around the circle's edge until you feel it is firm.

From the centre look around, aware of north, south, east and west, connecting the directions and elements. When you are ready, add the seasons of the year and the cycle of the day. Then, going back to the circle's edge, walk along those cycles, noting the changes that occur with every step you take the shifts in temperature, the changing colours and light.

When you feel sure that your circle is marked with these cycles, return to the centre and sit quietly for a while. When you are ready, think of an emotion or a desire, such as being tired, sociable, creative. Taking one at a time and without thinking, walk from the centre to the point on the circle's edge where you feel this state most strongly. If you truly allow yourself to move without first working out where you 'should' go, the results can be surprising, revealing areas where you are sustaining stress because you are not working with your natural highs and lows. Are you forced to be in company when you would rather withdraw? When would you naturally like to eat, or sleep? How do the cycles correlate, and how do these tie in to the directions and elements?

When you have finished the exercise, return to the centre and relax, centring yourself in your spirit energy, your strength. Then gently breathe in your aura circle until you are comfortable and give thanks to the spirits of place.

Sun and moon

To our ancestors, the moon, as well as the sun, was of vital importance, and there is evidence that ancient Druids' calendars were moon oriented. For those practising Druidry today, the moon is equal in importance to the sun and as many rites are held at night, in the flickering light of the fire, as are held during the daytime.

Understanding the relationship between sun, moon and Earth is a source for much spiritual adventure. What is the relationship between light, dark and bright, between source, reflection and perception, between reason, emotion and actuality. It is up to each individual to create and nurture his own unique relationship with the spirit energy of sun and moon.

Star markers

By the time the Celts reached Britain in the first millennium BCE the climate was not conducive to starwatching. None the less for many Druids there is a strong connection between their faith and the ancient tombs, standing stones and circles that align with the rising and setting of the sun, moon and various stars. Few in Druidry, however, practise in a high ceremonial style where the exact positions of stars are required in order to perform rites. For the modern Druid the goal is to attune with nature, slide in and extend our experience of its reality.

Stars are considered to be omens and guides rather than dictators of fate, our observation being an act of reverential awe and learning. The Druid strives to understand more fully all the energies – of the planets, stars, moons, gravity – which influence our journey. As through spirit every aspect of our world is connected, so the stars breathe their energy over our Earth through a cosmic web of connectedness.

Many Druids understand the skies sufficiently to work with the stars, constellations and planets as they change throughout the year, painting them into the changing colours of their temples and devotions.

Birth to death

The cycle of life is also played out within the sacred circle, its shades painted onto the circle's edge. So, as the sun begins its new journey in the depths of darkness at Midwinter, the new soul comes into life.

When the sun begins to rise higher, warming the earth, and shoots creep through the soil, so the infant grows into the child and with spring he emerges from the enfolds of his mother. Childhood adventures, growing consciousness and the development of independence are encompassed in the east. Adolescence takes us down towards the circle's south-east, where fertility and sexuality rise to a peak. In the south is the height of our physical expression, our creativity, where fire brings us courage, power and energy. Here is our adult life, which after Midsummer shifts towards middle age. As we move into the west, the emphasis on the physical is replaced by the importance of experience, wisdom and balance, the autumn leaves falling inevitably. The last period of our lives takes us into winter where death awaits us. At Midwinter we are reborn.

Attuning to the cycles of the natural world mirrors for us the cycle of our own lifespan. It reveals for us our perceptions and expectations of life, offering doorways of healing and adventure.

Paths of the circle

It isn't only the path around the edge of the circle that is used by the Druid. There are pathways that cross the centre, taking us down lines of reflection and connection that can offer poignant opportunities for healing.

In the east the child looks to the west, where the elder speaks his wisdom. In the west, as age creeps in, the soul looks to the child for a vision of freedom. In the south-east, where sexuality is humming, the couple looking for fertility acknowledge their ancestors in the north-west as they strive to create space for their descendants.

Just as places around the edge of the circle act as gateways into the deeper mysteries of the human psyche, so the paths across the circle do the same. The journeys we make through life take us to the cutting edges of our soul, where we grow in knowledge, beauty and certainty.

Animal lore

The spirits of the trees, shrubs and herbs that encircle our grove hold our energy, teach and inspire us, but it is the animal spirits that lead us into different worlds and levels of consciousness.

   Druidry is rich with teachings and guidance about the connections between the human soul and the animals around us. Some animals work simply as guides, enabling the Druid to expand his view of reality and travel further into other worlds. Others connect more deeply with the soul of the Druid and are known as totems. The totem animal will be one that has worked with the individual over many lives, remaining as an integral part of her soul's experience.

But how *does* an animal guide?
Through relaxing, listening, the soul slowly forms a relationship with an animal, making offerings, learning the language of spirit which both share. The seeker begins to see the creature in a new way, its move-ments, reactions, noises, all suggesting answers. The Druid may hear the voice of the creature in spirit, and through learning to access a profound level of empathy he can look at the world from its viewpoint.

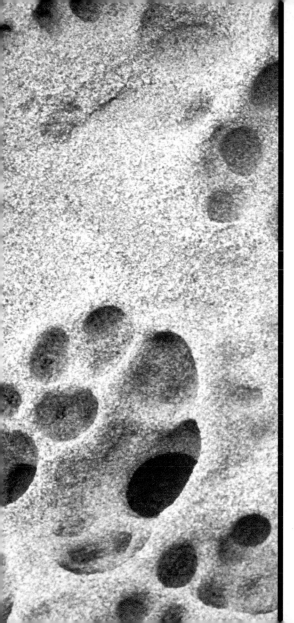

Each animal has its own strengths. For example, dogs are known for their loyalty, their understanding of leadership and rightful place in the pack, qualities that can be useful or self-negating. Through a relationship forged with a dog we find these aspects within ourselves, allowing a deeper healing, and offering healing to the dog through gratitude and respect.

In your own sacred space, having cast the circle of your aura and let go of distractions, find that state of being relaxed, listening. Become aware of yourself, how your emotions have coloured life recently, and consider what quality you would benefit from now. Strength, protection, calm, courage, playfulness … Then invite that quality to enter your circle in the form of an animal and let it happen in its own time.

Welcoming the creature, give offerings of thanks. Feel its energy. It is now up to you to nurture your relationship and learn from it.

Celebration

The importance of celebration in Druidry cannot be overstated. Eight major festivals celebrate the cycle of the year and, if rites of passage that mark important events in our lives are not woven into a festival rite, another celebration is declared to honour these too. Both are an expression of wonder at the natural world, enabling each soul to attune more powerfully to the significance of every step along the way.

Celebration strongly marks the importance of community. Though some in the tradition celebrate the festivals alone, an increasing number congregate, affirming the power of their rite and sharing laughter, strength and teachings.

So what are the festivals celebrated by modern Druids?

The festivals of the sun

Establishing a calendar at the latitude of the British Isles is best effected by the sun, watching the clear stretch in its path through the year from winter to summer. While other calendars may be created by the rising and setting of more distant stars, our climate doesn't allow such reliable sky watching. The dramatic shifts in light and temperature we experience through the year direct our focus to the sun, the source of the change. If you live in a more temperate climate, adapt the festivals to your own natural cycles.

Midwinter

In the cool temperate climate of Western Europe it is the rebirth of the sun at Midwinter, when the days start to get longer, that is seen by many in the tradition as the time of greatest celebration. The instinctive relief that the days are getting longer, that darkness has reached its peak, floods through the festival, secular, Christian and Pagan. Our Germanic ancestors, who called the festival Yule, established the tradition of celebrating for 12 days – one of many aspects of Paganism taken up by Christianity.

 In Druidry the Winter Solstice is celebrated around 21 December, when the sun enters Capricorn, or three days later on the date we call

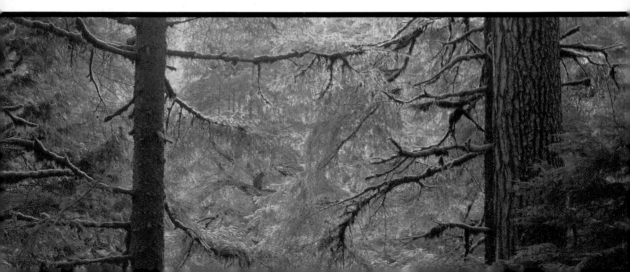

Midwinter, 24 December, when after a pause at its lowest point the sun once again starts its journey back towards the centre. Because in Druidry, as in Judaism, the day begins at dusk, celebrations kick off the evening before.

Midwinter is celebrated, as are all the eight and indeed most rites, with a ceremony held within the temple sanctuary of stones or wood or simply energy, where peace is affirmed and the circle cast, consecrated and blessed, and into which are invited the spirit presences, the ancestors and deities, with whom the Grove normally work.

The heart of the ceremony is the ritual ending of mourning for the death of the light. The year that was drawn to its close with the onset of winter is left behind. A new world is emerging, albeit still enfolded in the arms of its dark mother: her energy still surrounds us. With reverence we acknowledge her and her gift, the infant light.

Folk customs may be incorporated into the ceremony or the celebrations around the fire and the feast afterwards, including the burning of the winter oak log symbolizing the spirit of the hearth fires that warm the community. Mistletoe is distributed, carrying its magical blessings of healing, fertility and presence. Presents are given, expressing the energy of our spirit, honouring the new year and affirming bonds of love and community. This is often an intimate celebration, a time of caring, sharing and feasting with our close friends and family around us.

Spring Equinox

The Spring Equinox is celebrated between 20 and 23 March, on the date when the sun moves into Aries and day is the same length as night. It is a time of new life, daffodils and cherry blossom, fledglings, lambs running in the fields. The symbolism of the egg is prominent at this time. It is a time of celebration of childhood. It is also another turning point in the year. The darkness is behind us and ahead is the light into which we can grow.

The core of this ceremony is the blessing of seeds that will become the year's harvest. On a practical level, seeds might be blessed and sown in pots to be cared for at home – part of the work of caring for the land which each Druid takes part in.

Now the Sun Child has grown and his heat is touching the Earth, drawing us up into growth. In the rite this is often played out by the spring maiden and young sun god, aware of their sexuality yet not old enough to use it. They dance, not touching, shy and innocent, filled with the energy of life renewed. The festival is filled with laughter and anticipation as the balance tips towards the light.

Midsummer

The Summer Solstice is the festival most often associated with Druids, though it is of no more importance in the tradition than any other festival. It is celebrated around 21 June when the sun rises at its most northern point, or on Midsummer's Day three days later on 24 June, after the pause when the sun begins its descent.

The festival is a celebration of the peak and the further north we travel the more potent is this rite. The sun born at Midwinter has pushed back the powers of darkness to just a few night hours. But in the process he has exhausted himself (in many solar myths he is wounded in the fight) and it is at this point that his hold relaxes. Darkness once again begins to creep silently in.

The interplay of the forces of nature continues, weaving threads of tension, life and death, dark and light, male and female. Midsummer is a time of honouring the power of the light, the masculine, the mountain top, the sword's blade, the outer and assertive. Both qualities exist within every soul and are expressed in the changing flows of life; at this time we acknowledge the outward expression of ourselves, our vitality and strength, all we have used in the push for growth and progress, and we learn when to stop.

The celebrations often begin at dusk the evening before and include three distinct parts: the rite that initiates the night vigil, the rite of dawn and that of noon. First there is high celebration of the power of the Sun King and thanks and honour are given. At dawn the power of the sun is honoured with awe and offerings. The rite then changes at noon, as the turning tide is acknowledged. Our attention is drawn from the light that glints off the sword to the Earth, the goddess of our land.

Autumn Equinox

The Autumn Equinox is celebrated between 20 and 23 September, when the night is as long as the day once again. The balance is more poignant at this time than in the rush of spring and this is often the quietest of the festivals. The harvest is in; it is a time of acceptance of all we have and what we lack, a time of reflection on what we have achieved. The element of water is strong, the ebb and flow of the ocean tide, as we stand in the west of our sacred circle, reaching out to understand the mysteries of balance. This is a time of sharing gifts of abundance and strength, a time when participants bring to the rite offerings and presents for each other and the gods.

At many Groves it is usual to bless and share food and drink at all the festival rites. This is often in the form of a large round loaf of homebaked bread and honey mead (or cider, ale or wine) passed around the circle in a drinking horn. After giving thanks to the goddess of the land and to the lord of light, the gathering will ask for their blessings on the loaf and the horn. The first break of bread, the first drink of mead are given back to the land, to Mother Earth, the spirits of place, and if appropriate for the rite more is given to the ancestors.

The festivals of the seasons

While the solar festivals are fixed points in the cycle of the year, the other four mark the opening of a season. The energy of each of these festivals is evident throughout the three months that follow until the next one looms, altered by the solar turning point in the middle. Within Pagan Druidry, the seasonal festivals are most commonly known by the Irish Gaelic names Samhain, Imbolc, Beltane and Lughnasadh. They are also known as quarter days or lunar or fire festivals.

Samhain

For those who measure by the seasons, Samhain (pronounced *sow-inn*) arrives with the first frost. Some plan their rite around the full moon of Scorpio that passes through Taurus. Those who work around a consistent date celebrate Samhain on 1 November, with the rites beginning the evening before.

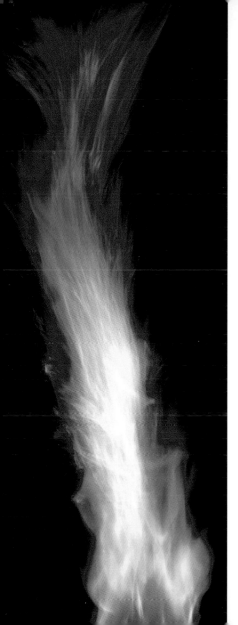

Traditionally at Samhain, livestock that would not last the winter were slaughtered with ritual thanks. Samhain marks the end of summer. It is a time of sacrifice. Ahead is the winter and decisions need to be made as to what we will carry through the long cold months, what will not survive, and what must be protected and nurtured as the source of next year's wealth.

So the festival rite is a process of letting go, beginning with an acknowledgement of what we have gained, how we have changed and who we have become, and followed by a period of mourning, knowing what we must release – and effectively letting it go. At this time, those who have died during the year are honoured and gifts are given with love and thanks. Our ancestors are invited to share and the feast is blessed and offered to the Earth, the spirits and all in the circle. Then the darkness of winter is welcomed in and a period of release is declared – bonfires are lit, the Summer King burnt, fireworks set off and the feasting begins.

Imbolc

By the calendar Imbolc (pronounced *im-olk*) is celebrated on 2 February. It is thought to refer to the ewes' milk which flows as lambs are born. Some mark the time of Imbolc by the birth of the first lambs, while others look for the first snowdrops.

This is the first festival of spring, when the Sun Child born in the depths of winter lifts his face and the Earth is touched with the first rays of warmth. The fire of Imbolc is the tender light of new life that flickers in the candles of the rite, the forge of the metal-working goddess who cleanses and re-forms our souls ready for the year ahead.

For many Druids Imbolc is the only festival entirely focused on the feminine deity and the rite is often powerfully gentle, woven with poetry, the circle veiled in white, expressing the innocence of the child. At this time we honour our mothers, and our mothers' mothers, with offerings of thanks to all who have given us life. Plans are shared, our aspirations and dreams, still abstract and wrapped in hope. White candles, planted in a cauldron of earth or water (symbolizing the body of the goddess or the waters of the womb), are blessed and lit, infused with our love, devotion, dreams and prayers.

Beltane

This is the first festival of summer, celebrated on 1 May, on the full moon of Taurus as it passes through Scorpio, or with the first pinky white blossoms of the hawthorn tree, also known as the may.

   The Beltane rite focuses on fertility: for those wanting children, for the land, for our own souls and dreams. The twin fires of the rite express the tension of opposites craving union, the source of creativity. The Earth has come alive now with energy bright and strong. The Sun King and the Spring Maiden have grown to sexual maturity and the ritual is the dance of their coming together. She is now the May Queen, with a crown of hawthorn, and he comes to her as the Lord of the Wildwood. Their dance is infectious, encouraging all who have gathered to leap the flames and be blessed.

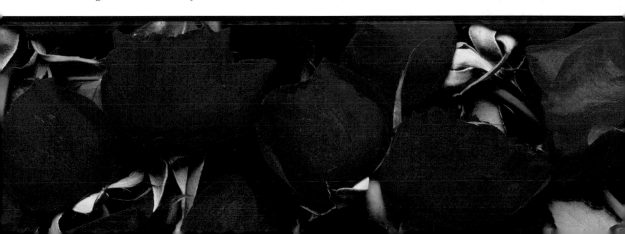

Lughnasadh

Lughnasadh (pronounced *loo-nass-ah*), is the festival of the god Lugh. It is the celebration of the first harvest of our local staple grain, usually wheat or barley. Some hold their rites on the full moon of Leo as it passes through Aquarius. By the calendar Lughnasadh is 1 August.

The season of growth since Beltane has come to its end and now we enter the season of reaping. Myths are often played out during the Lughnasadh rites, with the Corn King offering himself up to be sacrificed and being reborn as the loaf of newly baked bread. The sacrifice of the king was at one time very real, as blood was offered back to the gods who had given the grain. The focus of the rite

now is still this weave of exuberant life and release to death. It is both a celebration of what we have sown and nurtured, and an acknowledgement of its dying as it gives itself up to our needs.

Lughnasadh is often the biggest of the festivals, with people travelling from far and wide to share the joys of their harvest, bringing music and food, and trading crafts and stories.

One of the festivals will be coming up in the next month or so from the time of your reading this chapter. Which one is it? What season are we in? What is happening to the energy of the land and how does that relate to the energy of your body and soul? How would you like to celebrate the coming festival?

Rites of passage

The cycle of festivals allows us to take distinct steps through the year, acknowledging the changes and our own progress every six weeks. It is also felt necessary within the tradition to make clear statements of our progress through the cycle of our lives. So the Druid family is offered rites of passage which carry the members from conception to death.

These ceremonies of celebration, dedication and transformation are to some extent individually crafted to be specifically relevant to the people involved. They are designed to aid change, to bring confidence and affirm support. The newly conceived foetus is blessed, the new-born child welcomed, children are blessed with the falling of their first tooth and at other stages, most critically at puberty. Rites of marriage are marked, and at the farther side of life is the rite of elder. Rites of dying, death and mourning are also practised, working through the processes of healing, honouring and releasing with a profound under-standing of the spirit's continued consciousness after leaving the body. Many of these ceremonies can be performed publicly in such a way that family and friends, both Pagan and non-Pagan, can participate.

Rites of initiation

Rites of passage take place all through the journey into the tradition: the process of becoming a Druid is a lifelong experience. There is no hierarchy of initiatory grades which one can or must pass through in order to increase one's status or access to teachings. There is no end point.

Pledging with sincerity a personal commitment to the land, to the tradition, to one's ancestry is a profound step which in itself takes the individual through gateways into new spiritual perspectives. Many Groves and Orders offer a rite of initiation that marks the step into that group, this often being woven together with a personal commitment to the journey, a dedication to change and awaken.

On a deeper level, initiation happens as a result of having passed through doorways which activate a significant shift in consciousness. Walking through these boundaries often requires breaking through intense fear. The rite of initiation will then follow the experience, as an acknowledgement and thanksgiving to the forces who have guided us.

As with all rites of passage, initiations may be done both privately, between an individual, her guides, gods and ancestors and the spirits of the land, or with her Druid teacher, or more publicly, witnessed by a Grove or the wider community. Each is considered equally valid.

The Gods

Our teachers

Before long, anyone studying the faith with dedication will feel the presence of ancestral Druids, clarifying her vision in a way that increases awareness, revealing how it is the practice of Druid ritual and perception that is our most potent teacher.

   With no scripture to refer to, Druids also learn to communicate, in words or feelings, with the spirits of nature and these too guide us, revealing not simply their own lore and power but taking us deeper into ours. In accessing abilities to empathize with animals, perhaps even to shapeshift, the Druid learns tough and important lessons in equality and tolerance. Yet more powerful are the elementals, the spirits of the winds, rains, rivers, oceans, rocks and storms, fires and lightning. Their very being reveals to us areas of our psyche, our emotional and instinctual bodies, our beliefs and expectations, that would otherwise be veiled in the subconscious, and by relating to them more closely, we heal and regenerate.

Together with our ancestors, these spirit beings are potentially a source of that perfect inspiration at the heart of Druidry. Indeed, some look no further. If the goal of the journey is the exquisite joy of accessing the highest inspiration and its perfect expression through beauty, power and knowing, then surely all the powers of nature are enough.

But others look beyond these forces – to the realms of the gods.

What are gods?

Whether gods are merely archetypes, particular tones of life energy, or real entities, brings us back not to a debate but simply to restate that both these attitudes are found amongst modern Druids. Either way, the notion of deity describes a source of power.

Deities can indeed be purely elemental forces and powers of nature. Here we are simply referring to the vibrational 'intelligence' of hills, lakes and hurricanes as 'gods' instead of 'spirits'. At some point during our evolution our vision of these energies developed into form. The more powerful spirits became deities, some taking on animal characteristics, some blending animal with human and others becoming fully human images.

There are also gods who relate more closely to the human psyche than the natural world outside it. These too are forces of guidance, strength, validation and power, and are usually associated with our ancestors. More often than not, in their dealings with the human race they are seen in human form and the teachings they offer typically emphasize those of the ancestors: they are the gods of our ancestors. Reverence for these gods strengthens the continuity and development of our bloodline and our tradition.

The gods of our ancestors

Enough evidence remains to give us a fairly clear picture of the deities of these islands between the middle of the first millennium BCE and the medieval era, though how much Druids themselves had to do with these gods we cannot be sure. Most probably, while people had their own individual deities, of their family, hearth, local environment, their craft and ancestors, all of whom would be reverenced with prayers, offerings and small-scale sacrifice, Druids would have been summoned for anything more important.

Archaeology has revealed iconography from Bronze and Iron Age Europe, particularly southern Britain and France, that suggests a focus on deities of the sun, thunder, water, hunting and battle, and a common theme of a triple goddess. The Celtic culture was widely non-literate and it was not until the Roman invasion that altars and statues started bearing names. Yet still such an enormous number of deities are represented that any attempt to reconstruct a religious system becomes quickly tangled, taking us back to the understanding that deity was more about the spirit of place than some wider social order.

The gods of modern druids

With local gods and spirit guardians overwhelmingly the most common form of deity for our ancestors, the deities of the local environment are still the principal focus of devotions amongst dedicated Druids today.

However, many look back to find the gods of the old tribes too and medieval literature offers information about many of these deities, both the spirits of place and the mythical heroes. It is difficult to correlate the mythology in the literature with the archaeological finds and the Classical evidence. This also reveals the problems of working with texts so profoundly influenced by other cultures, not least the Christian. None the less, Druids who now wish to work with Celtic gods other than their local spirits of place will find many books that reveal their stories. Here I offer only a brief outline (there are recommendations for further reading on page 89).

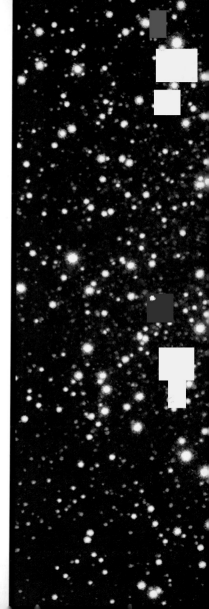

British gods

Of the key figures, one of the most commonly invoked in modern Druidry is Arianrhod, daughter of the mother goddess Don and of Beli Mawr, from whom all medieval dynasties claim descent. She is a goddess of the stars, in particular the constellation Corona Borealis. She is called the Lady of the Silver Wheel, and rules over birth and initiation. Her lover is Gwyddion, one of her brothers. He is a lord of the skies – the Milky Way is Caer Gwyddion – and a god of words, a Bard.

'Lleu of the Skilful Hand' is a god of many skills and a favourite amongst modern Druids. Manawyddan, a god of the sea, was married to Rhiannon, the horse goddess and so also a goddess of the land. Her first husband was Pwyll, Prince of Dyfed and a lord of Annwn, the underworld. The god of the underworld is Arawn, a hunter of souls who rides his grey horse through the dusk with his pack of white hounds with alarming red ears. Bran is a guardian of the land and a god of war, while his sister, Branwen, is a goddess of love and death.

Cerridwen, holder of the cauldron of inspiration and rebirth, is a dark mother goddess and possibly the most important goddess in the Welsh medieval literature.

The Irish gods

Many of the Irish gods now revered within Druidry are of the Tuatha de Danaan, the Children of Danu, a superhuman race who at Beltane in some year of prehistory conquered the Fir Bolg and took the island as their own. When later they themselves were overwhelmed it is said that the Tuatha disappeared into the sacred hills of the Earth where they became the faeryfolk, the Sidhe.

Dagda is the father god, known as the Good God and Lord of Knowledge. He is coarser than the other members of the Tuatha de Danaan. Dressed as a peasant, pot-bellied and dragging a vast club set on wheels, he is lord of life and death, offering abundance and rebirth from his vast cauldron of plenty. In many ways similar to the Dagda, yet younger and more refined, is Lugh, the 'shining' god. Lugh's son is Cu Chulainn, one of the great mythical heroes of the Irish texts.

Danu or Dana is a mother goddess of the land and a river goddess. Her name means 'sacred gift' and for some within the tradition it is used in the same way as the Welsh word *awen*, denoting inspirational energy. Among the other Irish gods, Bile is a god of death, some say husband to Danu. Mannanan Mac Lir is the sea god. Goibhnui is god of smithcraft and beermaking, similar to the Welsh Govannon.

Other gods

Not all modern Druids who work with non-local deities honour those of the Irish or British myths. The old Gallic gods are also acknowledged in some parts of the tradition. Esus, whose name means 'lord' or 'master', is said to be god of the sacred oak. Cernunnos, a horned fertility god, is one of the most popular gods in modern Paganism, while many Druids revere the Saxon gods, such as Woden and Freyja.

An important element in the tradition is the goddess of the land, in particular through her relationship with the king. If the bond between them was strong, the goddess would bless the land with abundance, but if he dishonoured her she would cause devastation. There are many stories in both the Irish and Welsh texts of how the bond between goddess and king was made.

The connection between horses and the goddess of the land is also common. One of the best known myths is that of Pwyll who, sitting on the mound of Arberth, is captivated by the sight of Rhiannon riding past on her white mare. The ancient chalk figure at Uffington, Wiltshire, is a particularly sacred place for many Druids, its white horse symbolizing the essential power of the land.

Perfect exchange

Relationship is the key to the way Druids work with their deities. While there is clear acknowledgement of the gods' power, there is no sense of hierarchy between gods and humankind. A Druid will strive to enchant a deity with whom she'd like to work. Giving offerings of reverence to nature and to the ancestors, she will endeavour to remain open, listening, waiting for a god or goddess to come to her. After the connection has been made, the process is then about building a strong relationship, learning through respect to understand the divine power and learning through devotion how she can give to that god of herself.

There is surrender, yet no sense of submission. The Druid will be uncovering too, through a growing clarity and consciousness, what it is that she wants. It may be protection, love, security, freedom, healing, teaching. But more often than not, within the tradition nothing more specific is requested than simply inspiration. The Druid knows that, with the gift of divine inspiration received, she will have all she needs: the idea or solution and the energy to make it happen.

To fully accept any gift, though, we need to have given sufficiently in return. Our relationships with the gods are built on this need for perfect exchange. We offer of ourselves, through both sacrifice and joy, giving back to the gods the creativity born of our inspiration. As our offerings are accepted, so we succeed in holding the attention of the deity, thereby nourishing the relationship. And as the relationship develops, the flow of divine energy that we are offered also grows, as do our love and trust, together with our ability to give … and to receive.

The experience of communion, of sharing energy with spirit, of opening to receive the *awen*, intensifies the Druid's perception and experience of the worlds within which she lives, because of the heightened awareness caused by the increased flow of energy. This in itself opens the mind to different levels of reality, broadening the perception and experience of life as a whole.

Useful Addresses

This introductory book provides only a brief glimpse of the richness of Druidry. Should you wish to explore further, the books listed below give further insight. There are too many Groves and Orders in existence around the world to mention them all here. Listed below are some of the larger and more open Orders. It must be left up to the individual to judge whether any person they meet, associated with these or any other groups, shares their vision of Druidry and is worthy of their attention and resources. The reason for listing the Orders I do is because they are useful for making contacts, whether the seeker is looking for more information, for training or for open celebration that they can attend.

These are listed in alphabetical order:

The British Druid Order (BDO), run by the founder Philip Shallcrass and myself as joint chiefs, came into being in 1979. It organizes events, workshops, conferences and talks in Britain and around the world, including public and private ritual for rites of passage and the major festivals. It publishes books and periodicals, including *The Druids' Voice*. Contact: BDO, PO Box 29, St Leonards-on-Sea, East Sussex TN37 7YP, UK. www.druidorder.demon.co.uk

The Druid Clan of Dana is another international Order with many Groves world-wide. It operates as a part of the Fellowship of Isis, the largest goddess-centred network in the world. Contact: The FOI, Clonegal Castle, Enniscorthy, Eire.

The Druid College of Albion is a gathering of Druids from many Pagan Druid Orders which offers a correspondence course rich in Celtic culture and star lore. Students have a personal tutor to guide them through the training. Contact: BM Stargrove, London WC1N 3XX, UK.

The Gorsedd of Bards of the Isles of Britain organize public celebrations at the major festivals in Britain and around the world. Ceremonies are family affairs, open to followers of any tradition, held in the spirit of Druidry and include rites of passage, initiation into the Gorsedd and open eisteddfod. Contact: BDO, PO Box 29, St Leonards-on-Sea, East Sussex TN37 7YP, UK. In America, contact: The Bards of Caer Pugetia, PO Box 9785, Seattle, WA 98109, USA.

The Henge of Keltria, one of the larger American Orders, runs a correspondence course with a strong Celtic leaning. There are Groves across the country sharing the ceremonies and teachings of the Order. Contact: Henge of Keltria, PO Box 48369, Minneapolis, MN 55448-0369, USA.

The Order of Bards, Ovates and Druids (OBOD) is the largest Order world-wide, led by chosen chief Philip Carr Gomm, many of whose books are listed below. OBOD runs a correspondence course which runs through the three grades of the tradition, giving a sound and inspiring grounding for any study of Druidry. Students are supported by a tutoring system. There are numerous Groves and groups which meet regularly all around the world, each with its own character and focus. Contact: OBOD, PO Box 1333, Lewes, East Sussex BN7 1DY, UK. www.obod.co.uk

Further Reading

Emma Restall Orr, *Spirits of the Sacred Grove* (Thorsons, 1998): a very personal weave of experiential Druidry and healing philosophy, revealing Druidry in its many colours.
Emma Restall Orr, *Ritual: A Guide to Life, Love and Inspiration* (Thorsons, 2000): the fine art of ritual explored and explained wth guidance allowing the reader to create their own rituals for every occasion.

Druidry
Philip Carr Gomm, *Elements of the Druid Tradition* (Element Books, 1991): a short book doing much the same as this one, only with a different style and focus.
Philip Carr Gomm, *The Druid Way* (Element Books, 1993): a journey through the Sussex countryside, weaving Druid history, philosophy and experience with psychotherapy.
Philip Carr Gomm (Ed.), *The Druid Renaissance* (Thorsons, 1996): a fascinating collection of articles written by prominent members of the Druid community.
Ross Nichols, *The Book of Druidry*, edited by Philip Carr Gomm and John Matthews, (Aquarian, 1990): it is quite a tome but filled with genuine eccentricity and interest.

Animals
Philip and Stephanie Carr Gomm, *The Druid Animal Oracle* (Simon & Schuster, 1995): a divination deck filled with animal lore and mythology, with illustrations by Bill Worthington which make it worth its weight in gold.

Myths

Jeffrey Ganz, *The Mabinogion* (Penguin, 1976): one of the best translations of this key text of Welsh medieval literature.

Jeffrey Ganz, *Early Irish Myths and Sagas* (Penguin, 1981): equally good on the Irish myths.

Thomas Kinsella, *The Tain* (Oxford University Press, 1970): a great translation of the Irish epic.

John Matthews, *A Druid Source Book* (Cassell, 1996): featuring some medieval literature together with a good deal of the eighteenth-century revival material.

Philip Shallcrass, *The Story of Taliesin* (British Druid Order, 1997): a clear and vibrant, annotated version of this key text.

History

Miranda Green, *Exploring the World of the Druids* (Thames and Hudson, 1997): useful and accessible for history if rather inaccurate on modern Druidry.

Ronald Hutton, *The Pagan Religions of the Ancient British Isles* (Blackwell, 1991): one of the best texts on British Pagan history, if rather academic, blowing out all the romantic misconceptions.

Ronald Hutton, *Stations of the Sun: A History of the Ritual Year in Britain* (Oxford University Press, 1996): the only work available which so comprehensively deals with this issue.

Prudence Jones and Nigel Pennick, *A History of Pagan Europe* (Routledge, 1995): a well written text which covers all of Europe and a must if you can't face Ronald Hutton's *Pagan Religions*.

Anne Ross, *Pagan Celtic Britain* (Routledge, 1967): a classic.

Trees

Ellen Evert Hopman, *Tree Medicine, Tree Magic* (Phoenix, 1992): an interesting and well crafted book on tree lore and Druid spirituality.

Ellen Evert Hopman, *A Druid's Herbal* (Destiny Books, 1995): as above, on herbs.

Jacqueline Memory Patterson, *Tree Wisdom* (Thorsons, 1997): a beautiful and informative book on trees and Druidry.

Liz and Colin Murray, *The Celtic Tree Oracle* (Rider, 1988): a divination set with useful tree lore.

Nigel Pennick, *The Secret Lore of Runes and Other Ancient Alphabets* (Rider, 1991): runes and ogham and all the rest.

Other orders

Philip Shallcrass, *A Druid Directory* (British Druid Order, 1997): a regularly updated edition listing all the working Druid Orders and Groves in Britain, with many from around the world.